AMIRE BEN SALMI

I AM A LEADER

A COLLECTION OF POSITIVE AFFIRMATIONS FOR THE MODERN DAY LEADER

I AM - A LEADER
POSITIVE AFFIRMATIONS FOR THE MODERN DAY LEADER

Published by I AM Publishing

Copyright © 2023 Amire Ben Salmi

The author asserts the moral right under the Copyright, Designs and Patents Act 1988 to be identified as the author of this work.

All Rights Reserved. No part of this publication may be reproduced, stored in a retrieval system or transmitted, in any form or by any means without the prior consent of the author, nor be otherwise circulated in any form of binding or cover other than that which it is published and without a similar condition being imposed on the subsequent purchaser.

Copyright © 2023 Amire Ben Salmi
Interior and cover design by Lashai Ben Salmi
All rights reserved.

Paperback ISBN: 978-1-915862-93-8
Hardback ISBN: 978-1-915862-94-5

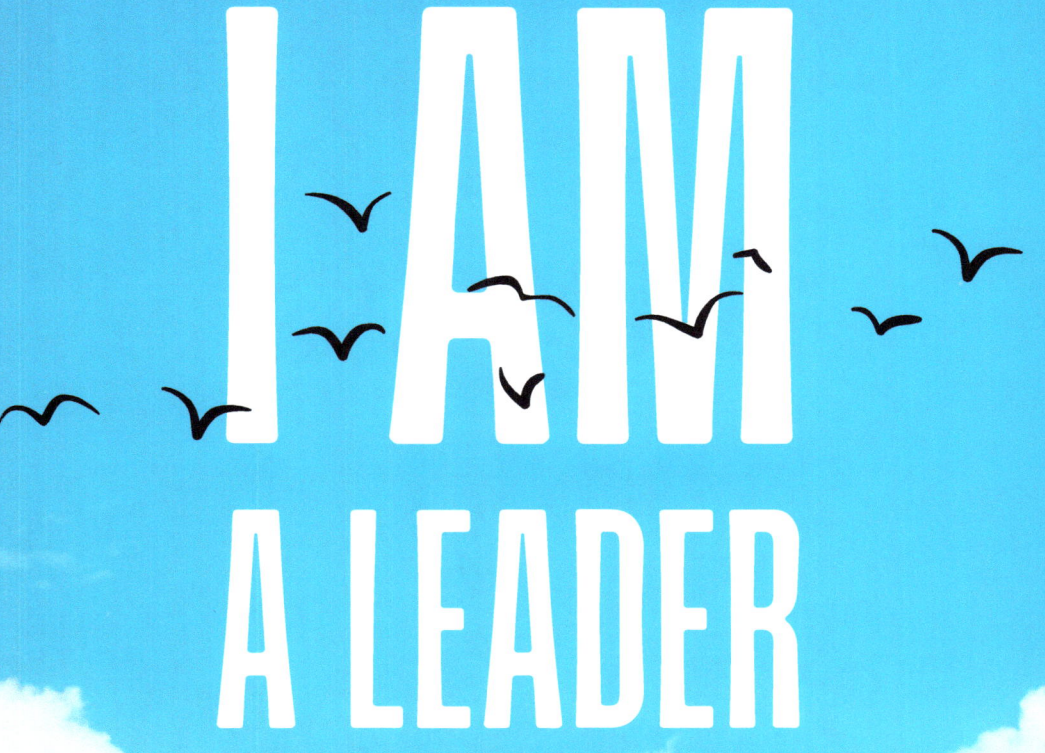

> "leadership starts with you

ACKNOWLEDGMENTS

ACKNOWLEDGMENTS

Dear Reader,

I want to take a moment to thank you for picking up this affirmation book on leadership. As a 9-year-old boy who is passionate about learning and leadership, I wanted to share my leadership affirmations with you. I was inspired to write this book after being invited to be a guest speaker by Carolyne A. Opinde Dr. h.c, founder of The NGO Whisperer Centre For Social Impact.

I would also like to thank my parents (Sabrina Ben Salmi and Mohamed (Amne) Ben Salmi, siblings (Lashai Ben Salmi, Tray-Sean Ben Salmi, Yasmine Ben Salmi, and Paolo Ben Salmi), nan (Mary Paul), Abuelo & Abuela (Alen Shelton & Justine Shelton), Rev Dr Trevor Adams, Apostle Linda Edwards, Rev Ezekiel Towobola, Grace Towobola, Lesley Warren, Prophet Frank Okyere and friends for always encouraging me to believe in myself and instilling the values of kindness, fairness, and responsibility. They are the reason why I'm able to share my affirmations with you today.

I would also like to thank my teachers and mentors, who have inspired me to be a better leader and provided me with the knowledge and tools to develop my leadership skills.

Finally, I want to express my gratitude to you, the reader. It takes courage to take steps towards personal growth and development. By picking up this book, you have shown a commitment to your own personal growth, and I hope these affirmations will help you become the best leader you can be.

Thank you for your support and encouragement.

Sincerely,

Amire Ben Salmi aka Mr Intelligent

DEDICATIONS

DEDICATIONS

To all the future leaders out there,

I dedicate this affirmation book to you! As a 9-year-old boy who loves to learn and explore, I know how important it is to have positive beliefs about yourself and your abilities. That's why I've filled this book with powerful leadership affirmations that will help you become the best leader you can be.

Remember, being a leader isn't just about being in charge or telling others what to do. It's about inspiring others to do their best, taking responsibility, knowing when to say sorry, knowing when to ask for help, being kind and fair, and making good choices. With the affirmations in this book, you can build your confidence, develop your skills, and become a leader who makes a difference.

So go ahead, read these affirmations out loud, and believe in yourself! You are capable of great things, and I can't wait to see all the amazing things you will achieve.

With love and encouragement,

Amire Ben Salmi aka Mr Intelligent

INTRODUCTION

INTRODUCTION

Dear Reader,

Welcome to my affirmation book on leadership! My name is Amire Ben Salmi. I'm a 9-year-old boy who is passionate about leadership, STEM, public speaking, and advocating for children. I am also the founder of I AM Publishing House, passionate about mentoring and personal growth. I am on a mission to put a smile on the faces of one million people faces, starting with YOU!

I believe that everyone has the potential to be a great leader, and that's why I've created this book filled with positive affirmations to help you become the best leader you can be.

Leadership is not just about being in charge or telling others what to do. It's about inspiring others to be their best selves, being kind and fair, and making good choices.

In this book, you'll find affirmations that will help you build your confidence, develop your skills, and become a leader who makes a difference. I've written these affirmations based on my own experiences and the lessons I've learned from my parents, teachers, and mentors.

I hope that by reading these affirmations, you'll be inspired to believe in yourself and your abilities and to take action towards your personal growth and development.

Remember, becoming a great leader takes time, effort, and practice. With the help of these leadership affirmations, you can build a positive mindset and develop the skills you need to become the leader you want to be.

Thank you for joining me on this journey towards personal growth and leadership. Let's get started!

Sincerely,

Amire Ben Salmi aka Mr Intelligent

I am a leader, and I am capable of making a positive impact on the world.

I lead with empathy, compassion, and understanding.

I inspire and empower others to become their best selves.

I am committed to creating a culture of inclusivity and diversity.

I believe in the power of teamwork and collaboration.

I take
responsibility for
my actions and
decisions.

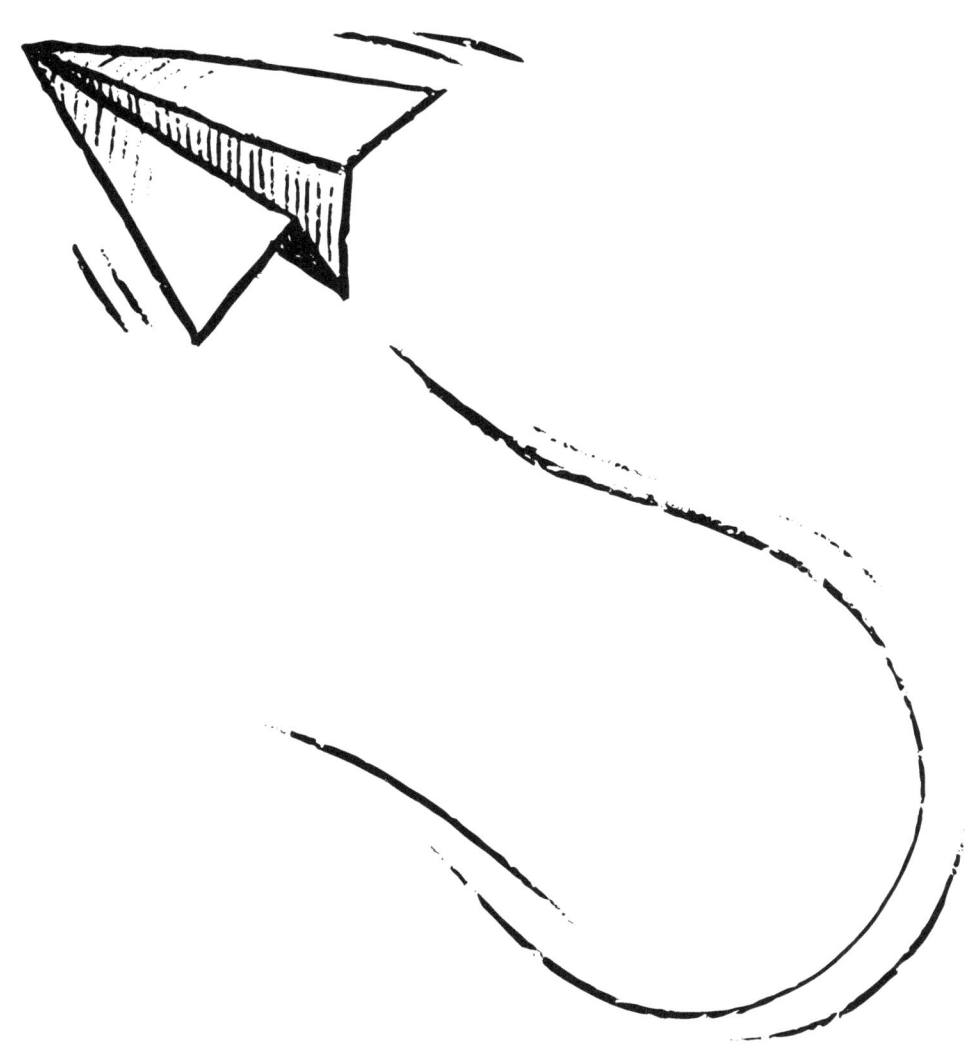

I am fearless in pursuing my dreams and goals.

I strive for excellence in everything that I do.

I am resilient and can overcome any obstacle.

I lead with integrity and honesty.

I am a visionary who sees possibilities where others see obstacles.

I embrace change and adapt to new circumstances.

I am a lifelong learner who seeks knowledge and growth.

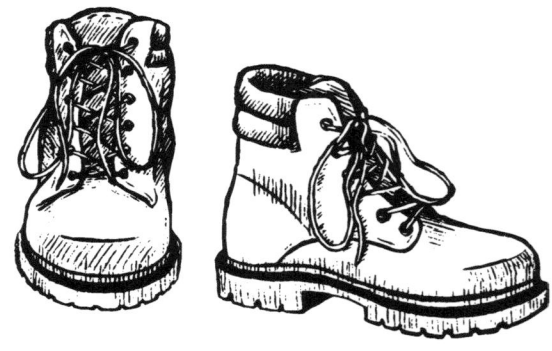

I am a mentor who guides and supports others on their journey.

I believe that anything is possible with hard work and determination.

I am the kind of leader who sees possibility everywhere.

I am a
positive
role model
for those
around me.

I understand that effective leadership requires continuous communication and feedback.

I am committed to creating a culture of trust and transparency in my leadership.

I am willing to take responsibility for my mistakes and learn from them.

I lead with a sense of purpose and vision for the future.

I inspire others to believe in themselves and their abilities.

I listen to the needs
and concerns of others
with an open heart
and mind.

I lead with compassion and empathy.

Every day is an opportunity to learn something new and become a better leader.

I believe in the power of teamwork and collaboration.

My purpose as a leader is to inspire and empower others.

I am open-minded and willing to listen to different perspectives.

I lead with integrity, honesty, and transparency.

I am constantly striving to improve myself and my leadership skills.

I am responsible for
my own success and
the success of those
around me.

I understand the importance of work-life balance and taking care of my well-being.

I treat everyone with respect and kindness, regardless of their background or beliefs.

I believe in the importance of creating a positive impact in the world.

I believe in the potential of every individual, and I work to help them reach their goals.

I lead by example and set high standards for myself and others.

I recognise and appreciate the contributions of others.

I am not afraid to take risks and try new things.

I understand that failure is a necessary part of growth and development.

I am committed to being a lifelong learner and seeker of knowledge.

I understand the importance of balancing compassion and assertiveness in my leadership.

I prioritise the well-being and happiness of those around me.

I believe in the importance of leading by example and demonstrating my values through my actions.

I communicate clearly and effectively with others.

I am constantly seeking feedback and constructive criticism to improve my leadership skills.

I embrace diversity and inclusivity in all aspects of my life and leadership.

I am open to new ideas and perspectives, and I encourage others to share their thoughts and opinions.

I believe success is achieved through hard work, determination, and perseverance.

I prioritise my mental and emotional well-being and encourage others to do the same.

I understand the importance of giving back to my community and positively impacting the world.

I am adaptable and flexible in the face of challenges and obstacles.

I recognise and celebrate the achievements of those around me.

I am dedicated to continuous learning and personal growth.

I lead with a sense of purpose and passion.

I am committed to being a role model for others.

I am honest with myself and others about my strengths and weaknesses.

I believe in the power of self-reflection and self-improvement.

I understand that leadership is not about power, but about service to others.

I am dedicated to creating a culture of growth and development in my leadership.

I believe that every individual has something valuable to contribute.

I lead with a sense of humility and gratitude.

I prioritise the needs and well-being of others before my own.

I am accountable for my actions and decisions.

I believe in the importance of building strong relationships with those around me.

I find solutions to problems that transform lives.

I am inspired to take leadership beyond that which I currently comprehend.

I am the kind of leader who knows when it is time to close my eyes, place my hand on my heart, take a deep breath to allow myself to release all that no longer serves me, and then inhale all that I need to carry on.

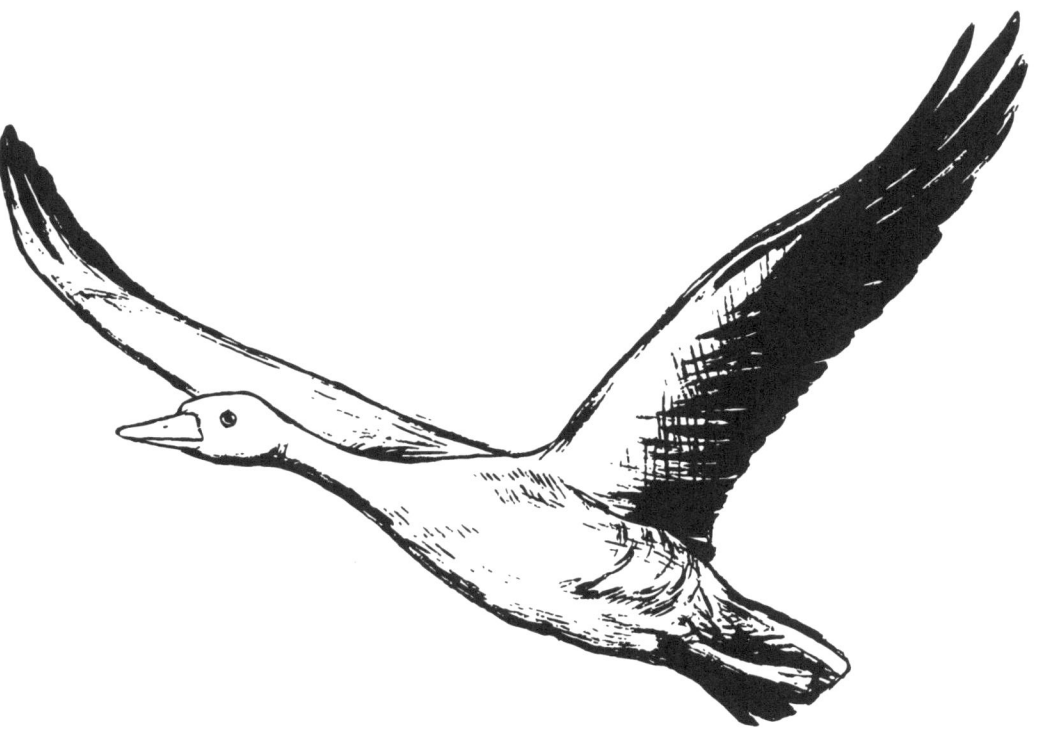

I am the kind of leader who loves to play, laugh, love and enjoy life.

I am a leader and I choose to inspire others to step into their power too.

Inside of my is the DNA of my ancestors and because of that fact I know that I am the answer to my ancestors prayers.

I am a leader and I pride myself in knowing when to ask for help and support to become the best that I can be.

I am capable of so much more than I can comprehend at this moment in time.

I am a leader and I choose to inspire others to step into their power too.

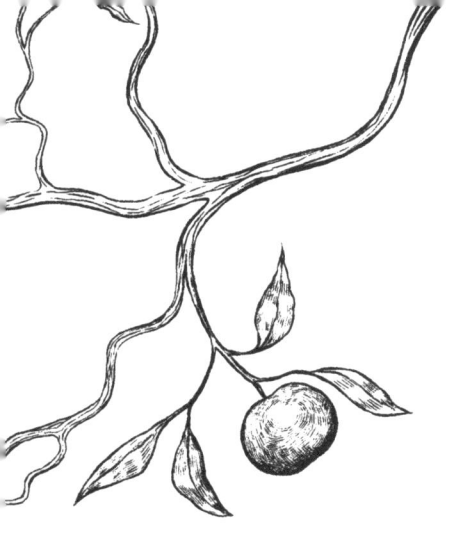

I am the kind of leader who sees strength in learning from everyone and everything in life.

Dear Reader,

As you close the pages of this leadership affirmation book, I want to leave you with a message of inspiration and motivation to take action towards becoming the leader you were born to be. Remember that leadership is not just a title or a position; it is a mindset, a way of being, and a set of actions you take daily.

To become a leader, you must first believe that you have the potential to lead. You must recognize your strengths and weaknesses and be willing to work on them. You must also have a clear vision of where you want to go and the courage to take the first step towards your goal.

Here are three action steps you can take right now to start your journey towards becoming a leader:

1. Develop a growth mindset: Embrace challenges and failures as opportunities to learn and grow. Seek out feedback and be open to constructive criticism.
2. Build strong relationships: Leaders need to be able to connect with others and build trust. Make an effort to listen actively, communicate clearly, and show empathy.
3. Take action: Leaders are not passive observers; they take the initiative and make things happen. Identify areas where you can take action and make a positive impact, no matter how small.
4. Remember, leadership is not a destination but a continuous journey of self-discovery, growth, and impact. Embrace the journey, stay committed, and never stop learning. Go forth and lead with purpose, passion, and integrity!

Sincerely,

Amire Ben Salmi aka Mr Intelligent

ABOUT The AUTHOR
MEET THE MIND BEHIND THE MISSION
HTTPS://LINKTR.EE/AMIREBENSALMI

AS HEARD ON THE RADIO & AS SEEN ON TV & IN NEWSPAPERS & MAGAZINES

Purpose: To put a smile on the faces of 1 Mission people faces starting with you through the teaching of affirmation

Amire and his family have planted their own fruit forest called the Ben Salmi Forest, located in Tanzania. Click on the link below to plant a tree in their forest:
https://forestnation.com/net/forests/bensalmifamilyforest/

Amire Ben Salmi also known as Mr. Intelligent is a 8-year-old award-winning author of a book series called: Because I AM Intelligent: Because I AM Intelligent - 365 Affirmations to Brighten Up Your Day, Because I AM Intelligent – Easy As P.I.E Affirmations and Because I AM Intelligent – I Become What I Affirm. 8-year-old Amire is the founder of I AM Publishing House. Amire is the youngest of the Ben Salmis 20-year-old Lashai Ben Salmi, 16-year-old Tray-Sean Ben Salmi, 13-year-old Yasmine Ben Salmi and 12-year-old Paolo Ben Salmi)

Amire is proud to be the youngest-ever honorary STEM Ambassador in history for Brunel University London (B.U.L). B.U.L has given homeschooled families the opportunity to participate in masterclasses for the first time in history, thanks to Lesley Warren. Amire and his family held their 2 Day signature family workshop called Dreaming Big Together - Mamas Secret Recipe at The Hub Chelsea FC and Virgin Money.

ABOUT The AUTHOR
MEET THE MIND BEHIND THE MISSION
HTTPS://LINKTR.EE/AMIREBENSALMI

9-year-old Amire is the founder of I AM Publishing House

Amire hosted his signature program called Because I AM Intelligent - Easy As P.I.E Affirmations held at Virgin and Chealsea FC.

BEN SALMI FAMILY MANTRA

"BEN SALMI TEAMWORK MAKES THE DREAMWORK

We believe that there is no such thing as failure, only feedback.

We also believe that the journey of one thousand miles begins with a single step in the right direction

FAMILY ANTHEM

If you want to be somebody,
If you want to go somewhere,
You better wake up and PAY ATTENTION

I'm ready to be somebody,
I'm ready to go somewhere,
I'm ready to wake up and PAY ATTENTION!

The question is ARE YOU?

Let's STAY CONNECTED
HTTPS://LINKTR.EE/AMIREBENSALMI

in — Amire Ben Salmi

◉ — @AuthorAmireBenSalmi

✉ — info@dreamingbigtogether.com

> ❝ BEING A LEADER DOES NOT ALWAYS MEAN THAT YOU HAVE TO LEAD FROM THE FRONT. TRUE LEADERS SHOW UP WHEREVER THEY HAVE TO, WHETHER FROM THE FRONT, THE MIDDLE OR THE BACK.

www.ingramcontent.com/pod-product-compliance
Lightning Source LLC
Chambersburg PA
CBHW041522090426
42737CB00037B/2